365 REASONS WHY BICYCLES MAKE THE BEST COMPANIONS

Dave Mosier

ATHENA PRESS

MIAMI   LONDON

ISBN 1 931456 34 8

First Published 2002 by
ATHENA PRESS PUBLISHING CO.
1001 Brickell Bay Drive, Suite 2202
Miami, Florida 33131

Printed for Athena Press

365 REASONS WHY BICYCLES MAKE THE BEST COMPANIONS

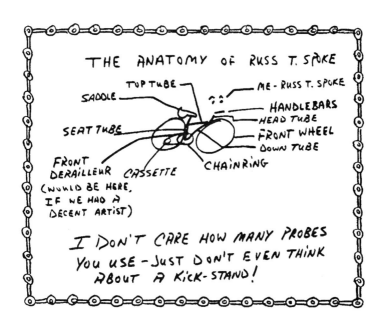

THE ANATOMY OF RUSS T. SPOKE

TOP TUBE
ME - RUSS T. SPOKE
SADDLE
HANDLEBARS
HEAD TUBE
SEAT TUBE
FRONT WHEEL
DOWN TUBE
FRONT DERAILLEUR
CASSETTE
CHAINRING
(WOULD BE HERE, IF WE HAD A DECENT ARTIST)

I DON'T CARE HOW MANY PROBES YOU USE - JUST DON'T EVEN THINK ABOUT A KICK-STAND!

Introduction by Russ T. Spoke

This work is dedicated to your sometimes gleaming, sometimes not, sometimes flying, sometimes flat, riding partners – your bicycles. It is true that some would have you believe that bicycles are simple, mechanical objects. *Those people* have no soul. *Those people* have never experienced the camaraderie of climbing to the top of the steepest hill with your bicycle and then screaming down the other side at such a pace that the birds are jealous. *Those people* have never ridden quietly through the park and come upon deer, fox, rabbit and occasionally a skunk. *Those people* drive too fast and take up too much of the road. This work compares the character traits of *those people* to the noble bicycle. The resulting conclusion from this comparison can only be that bicycles make the best companions.

So sit back (or lean forward on your drop handlebars if you're more comfortable) and see if your bicycle shares some of the following characteristics.

Before you get started, a non-mechanical friend of mine wanted it clearly understood that this work is really about bicycles. *Those people* might misconstrue some of the less flattering comparisons that follow. There should be no misinterpretation. Any resemblance to *those people* or any other person, living or otherwise, is purely coincidental. Besides, this is a work about bicycles. It would be vain of you to think that non-bicycles were the primary focus of *365 Reasons Why Bicycles Make the Best Companions*.

January

1

Your bicycle generally has no problem obeying posted speed limits and, if it does exceed the limit, instead of tickets, it receives medals.

2

Your bicycle will never forget that it made no objection when you invested in the dot.com IPO.

3

When someone says, "Your bicycle is smokin'," it is a good thing.

4

When you meet a new bicycle you won't be arrested for running your hands over its top tube and checking its cable tension.

5

You won't get arrested when your bicycle starts screamin'.

6

When your bicycle goes flat, you can pump it up.

7

Your bicycle is always on time.

OH YEAH!
THE MONSTER BIKE RALLY

8

Your bicycle will not complain if you ride all day long.

9

Your bicycle will never forget your name during your first ride.

10

You can ride more than one bicycle a day and not feel guilty or have to make excuses.

11

Your bicycle always enjoys a quickie.

12

Your bicycle won't gain weight, except during a rainstorm.

13

Your bicycle won't wake you in the middle of the night because it heard a noise.

14

Your bicycle never has morning breath.

15

Your bicycle is never jealous of another bike's paint.

COBBLESTONE

16

It generally takes your bike fifty miles or more to be a pain in the ass.

17

Your bicycle will never recite verbatim a conversation from six months earlier.

18

As you journey down the road of life, your bicycle will not blame you for the potholes.

19

Your bicycle will appreciate the suggestion that its headlights be enhanced.

20

Your bicycle doesn't borrow money.

21

Your bicycle doesn't feel the need to make small talk.

22

Your bicycle's relatives will stay in the garage and will not drink your beer.

23

Your bicycle enjoys outdoor rides.

DAMN BIFOCALS

24

During a ride, your bicycle doesn't mind if you're thinking about other bicycles, food, or what you'll be doing after the ride.

25

Your bicycle hums on a good ride.

26

Your bicycle doesn't need to be reminded to shave.

27

Your bicycle doesn't try to understand you.

28

Your bicycle leaves its emotions in the garage (with its relatives).

29

Your bicycle never needs additional closet space for its pedals or seat covers.

30

Your bicycle never takes the blanket away from you in the middle of the night.

31

Your bicycle recognizes that there is only one captain on a ride and that's the person with the helmet.

February

1

Your bicycle will never tell you that it will go wherever you decide, and, when you announce the plan, respond, "And just when were you going to discuss this with me?"

2

You don't have to wine and dine your bicycle before a ride.

3

Your bicycle doesn't get jealous if you ride another bike.

4

You can always share your bicycle with your friends.

5

You can ride your bicycle in public in all fifty states and most foreign countries.

6

You don't have to pretend to listen to your bicycle.

7

Your bicycle will never mentally (or metally) undress you.

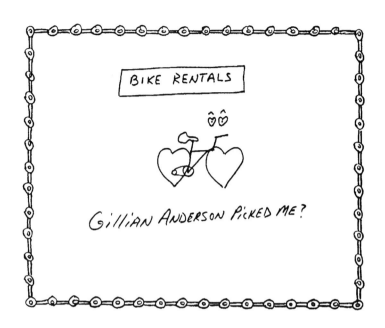

BIKE RENTALS

Gillian Anderson Picked Me?

8

Your bicycle never expects you to make arrangements for a Saturday ride by Wednesday.

9

When you first start riding your bicycle, its friends and family won't refer to you as the flavor of the month.

10

A new chain satisfies your bicycle's desire for jewelry.

11

Your bicycle doesn't use your credit cards.

12

Your bicycle will never tell a lie.

13

Your bicycle does not feel the need to ask probing personal questions to discover your innermost feelings. It's happy if you have an oil can, even if you aren't sure of how to use it.

14

On Valentine's Day, your bicycle prefers a good ride to thorny roses.

BICYCLE CHIROPRACTOR

15

Your bicycle doesn't expect you to cuddle after a ride.

16

Your bicycle doesn't pester you to hold it before you leave it in the garage (with its relatives) for the night.

17

Your bicycle doesn't stand between you and necessities – like food. Instead, your bicycle will gladly take you to these things at any time you desire.

18

Your bicycle never requires sweet whispering during a ride.

19

Your bicycle never asks you if you think it's getting fat.

20

Your bicycle doesn't complain about a rough ride.

21

Your bicycle never complains about lack of accessories.

22

Your bicycle never pesters you to stop and get directions.

23

Your bicycle doesn't nag you about anything, and certainly never about wearing your favorite lucky riding shirt.

24

Your bicycle is always grateful and is never offended when you notice and replace its worn or unsightly parts.

25

If you don't want to go for a ride, your bicycle does not accuse you of not loving it.

26

Your bicycle expects to ride on the roof of the car, on a trunk rack or in the back of the truck.

27

On a rainy day, your bicycle won't complain about your friends hanging around, drinking beer, playing cards, and watching the game.

28

On a sunny day, your bicycle won't complain about your friends hanging around, drinking beer, playing cards, and watching the game.

COMMUNAL SHOWER

March

1

On a sunny day, your bicycle won't nag you to stay home and mow the lawn.

2

Your bike won't blame the dog.

3

Your bicycle will never try to wear tires that are two sizes smaller than its rims.

4

Your bicycle will never threaten to relieve itself in your car if you don't stop at the next rest area.

5

If your bicycle has a padded seat, it is by design.

6

You never have to zip up the back of your bicycle's seat cover before you ride.

7

Your bicycle doesn't get mad when you laugh during a ride.

HEY! C'MON! GROUCHY RIDER,
HIDDEN POTHOLE IS GONNA' START

8

Your bicycle understands when you want to take a break during a ride for something to eat.

9

Your bicycle doesn't roll away when you refer to another bike during a ride.

10

Your bicycle doesn't get mad at you for commenting favorably about another bike's headlights.

11

Your bicycle doesn't stop riding because you suggest that it needs new fenders.

12

After you buy your bicycle a new chain on Friday, it doesn't expect you to buy new handlebar tape on Saturday.

13

Your bicycle does not expect that you will respond to its horn within ten minutes.

14

When you don't respond to your bicycle's horn within ten minutes, it doesn't assume that you are on another bicycle.

15

Your bicycle won't use your razor.

16

Your bicycle won't hang its fenders from the shower-curtain rod.

17

You can spend a weekend with your bicycle and still be happy to be bringing it home.

18

Your bicycle won't start crying when it's happy.

19

Your bicycle may take you to the shopping mall, but it will never expect you to go shopping.

20

Your bicycle will never expect you to watch *Bridges of Madison County*.

21

When your bicycle busts your stones, you at least know why.

22

Your bicycle won't check for another bike's grease on your clothes.

23

Your bicycle expects you to think lusty thoughts, before, during and after a ride.

24

Your bicycle will never lock itself out of the house.

25

Your bicycle doesn't need new tires to match your jersey.

26

Your bicycle does not try to analyze you – and then blame you because it doesn't understand you.

27

Your bicycle does not expect you to be in touch with your emotions.

28

Your bicycle doesn't unexpectedly show up.

29

Your bicycle will never chastise you because you don't communicate.

30

Your bicycle will never insult your taste in clothing by buying you a new wardrobe.

31

Your bicycle can communicate in all languages.

OH NO!
A GARAGE SALE TAG

April

1

Your bicycle looks good in the morning.

2

Your bicycle won't cop an attitude – about anything!

3

You can share some of your favorite entries from this list with your bicycle, laugh aloud, and still ride.

4

Your bicycle enjoys the same television and radio programs that you do.

5

Your bicycle doesn't know or care who Yanni is.

6

Your bicycle doesn't come to bed with curlers.

7

Your bicycle doesn't come to bed with cream all over its headset.

8

Your bicycle doesn't wear perfume that you can smell after it has ridden into the next county.

9

Your bicycle doesn't wear perfume that would kill roaches.

10

Your teenage bicycle never asks to borrow the car.

11

Your bicycle isn't a backseat driver.

12

You expect the "silent treatment" from your bicycle on a long ride.

13

Your bicycle doesn't pout.

14

Your department store, off-the-rack, assemble-yourself, generic bicycle does not try to convince you that it's a hand-crafted specialty bike by putting on extra handlebar tape and expensive lubricant.

15

Your bicycle doesn't get mad because you didn't notice or comment on its paint.

16

Your bicycle will never run another bicycle off the road to get its tricycles to soccer practice.

17

Your bicycle will never ask you to purchase a mini-van instead of a sports car.

18

If your bicycle were your daughter, it would never date anyone with no teeth that drives a suburban (us)ault vehicle*.

19

Your bicycle will never vote just to cancel out your vote.

20

No matter how wide the tire on your bicycle, it will never take other drivers for granted on the road or on the trail.

21

Your bicycle likes toys and gadgets.

22

Your bicycle feels no shame about riding alone.

---

* The uninitiated might think that the acronym "SUV" represents "sport utility vehicle". This is not the case. SUV stands for "suburban (us)ault vehicle." "S" for suburban, because this type of vehicle (you know the type – you can't see over it, around it or through it) is too big and clumsy to practically maneuver in city traffic. "U" for (us)ault because you and me (us), are constantly being assaulted by these vehicles. "V" for vehicle (and the word vehicle is used only to be polite) to refer to these dinosaurs of the road.

23

You never have to worry about being between your bicycle and a buffet.

24

Your bicycle won't pull into oncoming traffic to point out another bicycle's house.

25

Your bicycle keeps you feeling young and young at heart.

26

When your bicycle has a flat tire, it will stop. It won't keep riding along on the rim under some mysterious belief that by discussing the flat tire, it will fix itself.

27

Your bicycle doesn't always think that it knows best.

28

Your bicycle doesn't care that you have a little grease under your fingernails.

29

Your bicycle doesn't like potpourri.

30

Your bicycle knows the difference between a pitcher and a quarterback.

Hi, O SILVER (OR RED, BLACK...)

May

1

Your bicycle gets along with your mother.

2

Unlike your mother, your bicycle won't show silly baby pictures to total strangers.

3

Unlike your mother, your bicycle won't harp at you to pick up your socks.

4

Unlike your mother, your bicycle won't make you feel guilty, about anything.

5

Unlike your mother, your bicycle doesn't telephone and interrupt, or rather, wake you up, on a Sunday morning.

6

Unlike your mother, your bicycle doesn't care whether you have a steady riding partner.

7

Unlike your mother, your bicycle doesn't pester you about when it can expect a tricycle.

8

Unlike your mother, your bicycle doesn't visit and rearrange your living room, kitchen, and guest room.

9

Unlike your mother, your bicycle won't remind you how much it enjoyed the company of your last riding partner.

10

Your bicycle won't move the seat forward and then not bother to move it back.

11

When you are not riding, your bicycle will stay on its own side of the bed.

12

Your bicycle doesn't rub its cold pedals all over you to get them warm.

13

Your bicycle will never order lunchmeat by the slice.

14

Your bicycle will never plan to go camping with a group of other bicycles and, the night before the trip, ask you to pack everything it will need for the expedition.

IS THAT A TIRE LEVER
IN YOUR POCKET OR
ARE YOU JUST HAPPY THAT
WINTER IS OVER?

15

When your bicycle and the other members of the camping group finally get together, your bicycle will never ask you to pack a 100 cubic feet suburban (us)ault vehicle with 200 cubic feet of gear.

16

Your bicycle will never purchase lots of insurance coverage on you and then encourage you to ride without a helmet.

17

Your bicycle will never make you wait because it can't find a saddlebag to match its handlebar tape and chain.

18

Your bicycle will never pull a sanitary napkin out of its saddlebag in a restaurant.

19

When it comes to saddlebags, your bicycle realizes that less is more and more than necessary is too much.

20

Your bicycle will never expect you to comprehend how it can be a killing machine in the Army, but scared to death of a spider in the bathroom.

21

Your bicycle will always follow your directions.

NOW BE CAREFUL!
STAY ON THE SIDEWALK.
DON'T RIDE WITH STRANGERS
DON'T ACCEPT CANDY FROM
SUBURBAN (US)AULT VEHICLES

22

No matter how much you or anyone else compliments your bicycle, its headset will remain the same size.

23

Your bicycle doesn't pretend to be a psychologist because it parked in the stand outside a psychology lecture hall one semester. On the other hand, it can listen to your babbling for hours without interrupting and you always feel better afterward, so maybe it did learn something.

24

Your bicycle will never ask you to be its chauffeur and ride it to some silly ass event so that it won't be unattended.

25

Your bicycle may need parts repaired or replaced. The worn or damaged parts can be identified and in relatively short order your bike can be as good as new.

26

Your bicycle will never tell you that your relationship needs fixing and then, for as long as you can stand to listen, tell you all of your faults that cause problems with the relationship.

27

Your bicycle won't order cabbage rolls in a crowded restaurant and then, after dinner, announce that it has irritable bowel syndrome that is aggravated by cabbage.

EASTER BUNNY BIKE

NOT FUNNY!

28

Your bicycle won't tell you personal things about itself that you would rather not know (see May 27) and then expect you to prevent it from eating the cabbage.

29

After the event of May 27, you can make a quick, clean exit from the restaurant on your bicycle.

30

Your bicycle doesn't pretend to be a psychiatrist, although it is a good listener on long rides.

31

Your bicycle doesn't borrow your clothes.

CARE TO DANCE?
I WON'T ROLL ON YOUR TOES.

June

1

Despite casual dress codes, your bicycle is always properly outfitted; you can ride in a tuxedo or tight-fitting, metallic-colored clothing and you and your bicycle still make a good-looking couple.

2

Your bicycle has relatively straightforward operating mechanisms and appreciates your efforts, however feeble, to properly manipulate its power train.

3

Your bicycle is content to do nothing rather than undertake some activity just for the sake of engaging in the activity together, regardless of how painfully boring, tedious or offensive to the senses.

4

Even during the cold and flu season, your bicycle won't sneeze on you.

5

Your bicycle won't wake you up to ask if you were sleeping and then, when you politely try to go back to sleep, say, "Well, since you're awake now, let's talk."

THE HUMANS I WATCHED
SEEMED TO ENJOY THIS.
HEY! BE CAREFUL.
THAT'S MY DERAILLURE!

6

Your bicycle will never suggest that you go forward with some activity just because "it won't hurt you" or "it won't kill you to do that".

7

Your bicycle realizes that every ride is fraught with peril, especially if there is a possible encounter with a suburban (us)ault vehicle.

8

Your bicycle doesn't feel obligated to refer to you by anything other than your given name. It doesn't need to invent some term of endearment for the people who ride it. Just Velcro on your riding shoes and go.

9

You never have to be afraid that your bicycle will misinterpret anything you say.

10

Your bicycle will keep a secret.

11

Your bicycle will not tie up the telephone line when you want access to the Internet (to look at pictures of other bicycles).

ALRIGHT! SO I'M SLUMMING IT! BUT REMEMBER, THIS IS HOW THE SHUTTLE TRAVELS.

12

You will never have to buy new furniture to keep your bicycle happy. Your bike will be happy with a wall rack. However, for an interesting (and refreshing) change, give your bicycle the couch and use the wall mount for a non-bicycle creature that resides with you.

13

When you go on a trip, your bicycle can pack its gear into one saddlebag.

14

When you go on a trip with your bicycle, you don't have to stop at the outlet malls.

15

Your bicycle will never complain that a helmet should not be worn because it will clash with a riding outfit.

16

You don't have to explain to your bicycle why "helmet hair" is better than a cracked skull.

17

Your bicycle will never spend $100 for a haircut, excuse me, a style cut, which looks like the kid next door did the styling while trimming the hedges while his buddies waited on their bicycles so they could go for a ride.

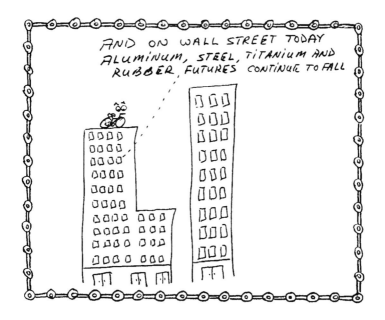

18

Your bicycle will never expect you to bite your tongue to withhold your laughter at its hedge-trimmed haircut.

19

Your bicycle doesn't use highlights in its hair, since it has no desire to model its appearance after a skunk.

20

Your bicycle won't subject you to its green egg tofu and wheat germ diet this month, and oranges, horseradish, and raisin diet next month.

21

Your bicycle will never use the VCR to record afternoon talk shows.

22

Your bicycle will never buy a soap opera summary.

23

To paraphrase Al Bundy (character from the popular TV series *Married With Children*, you can at least get scrap value for your bicycle.

24

To your bicycle, accessorizing means a manufacturer's insignia decal on the headset.

BICYCLE CATCHERS
ON SUBURBAN
(US)AULT VEHICLES!

25

Your bicycle can have embarrassing decals removed without plastic surgery.

26

Your bicycle doesn't demand to have a pet to keep it company and then require you to feed it, walk it, and clean up after it.

27

Your bicycle appreciates a good cigar, even if it doesn't smoke.

28

Your bicycle will ride with you even if you don't drive a Porsche or a BMW.

29

You can ride your bicycle to the nudie bar where your bike will wait patiently for you. You can ride without problems after the show.

30

You never have to worry about extra chairs when your bicycle's friend stays for dinner.

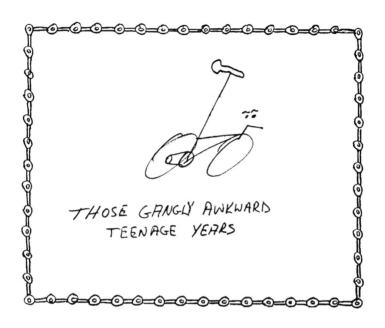

THOSE GANGLY AWKWARD
TEENAGE YEARS

July

1

Your bicycle will always share its handlebars during a séance.

2

When bicycles stay for dinner, they always have interesting stories from the road instead of boring vacation photos.

3

Your bicycle will never leave a make-up ring in the hot tub.

4

Your bicycle will never order a new teensy-weensy fanny pack and then complain that the neighbor has started to "bird-watch".

5

Your bicycle measures, watches, and detests every extra gram of weight.

6

Your bicycle will never voluntarily pierce its parts with sharp objects.

SO DOC,
CAN I RIDE THIS AFTERNOON?

7

Your bicycle enjoys being clamped in a sturdy, adjustable work stand in which it can be tipped, tilted, and rotated.

8

Your bicycle won't buy gasoline at prices over $2 per gallon – in fact, your bicycle won't buy gasoline at any price.

9

If your bicycle won the lottery, it wouldn't ride away without you.

10

Perhaps it's a coincidence, but your bicycle has the same driving habits as you.

11

Your bicycle will ride in the rain without mind-numbing chastisement that children would know better.

12

Your bicycle will never ask you to decorate your curbside with multi-colored cinders or cinders of any type that would endanger another bicycle's life.

13

Your bicycle doesn't just age; it becomes a classic.

14

Your bicycle will never ask a question and, before you can answer, inform you that "this would mean a lot to me".

15

Your bicycle will never punch its handlebars into a melon to determine if it's ripe and then return the damaged fruit to the produce stand.

16

Your bicycle will never ask a question and, before you can answer, advise you that "you better know what the answer is".

17

Your bicycle will never ask you to cuddle during an action/adventure movie.

18

Your bicycle will never see a motion picture five times.

19

Your bicycle is never threatening or overbearing; it is friendly and inviting.

20

If your bicycle were an engineer, it would design intersections so that you could see crossing traffic without having to "inch out" into the intersection.

21

If your bicycle were a city planner, it would never allow blind driveways.

22

If your bicycle were an engineer, it would never design roads with intersections just over the crest of a hill.

23

If your bicycle were an engineer, it would never design a road with a 90° turn at the bottom of a steep hill.

24

Your bicycle will never smell itself in an airport (swear to god – Russ T. Spoke watched a human smell herself in Detroit, Metro on 6/29/2000 at 4 P.M.). Your bike just would not do that anywhere.

25

Your bicycle will never fly with a stuffed animal that is larger than it is.

26

Your bicycle will never bitch about riding because it would rather be tanning.

27

Your bicycle will never force you out of the house because of a perm party with the other bikes in the neighborhood.

FAMOUS BICYCLE ARCHEOLOGIST

28

If your bicycle has a mechanical failure, it won't ride thirty miles out of the way and then call you and ask you what to do about the problem.

29

Your bicycle knows it has to read the owner's manual.

30

Your bicycle won't just walk the dog – it would race it!

31

Your bicycle will never ask you to chaperone a group of tricycles that are not accompanied by adult riders.

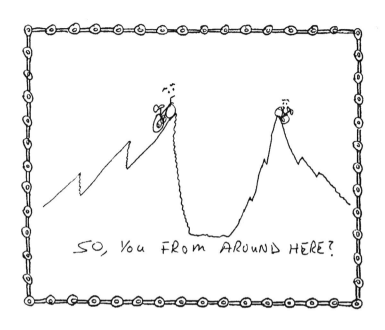

August

1

Your bicycle likes to have its tires rotated.

2

Your bicycle doesn't need any batteries to experience a good ride.

3

Your bicycle has never been convicted.

4

Your bicycle will never expect you to cuddle on the hottest, stickiest, sweatiest, most chokingly hot, humid night of the decade.

5

Your bicycle will never turn up the air conditioning to the maximum setting and then roll away with all of the covers.

6

Even if you were negligent during the ride, your bicycle won't sue you just because you have insurance.

Rock 'N Roll, LITERALLY

7

No matter how inept you are while lubing, cleaning, and otherwise maintaining your bike, it will never sue you for mechanical malpractice.

8

Your bicycle has developed real character from years of bike discrimination. For example, bicycles are still not allowed in most stores or office buildings. Nor are they allowed on many forms of public transportation. When entering many apartment buildings, landlords require that bicycles ride the service elevator.

9

Your bicycle can make left turns without first swerving to the right berm, and can make right turns without its wheels crossing the centerline.

10

Your bicycle understands that if it invests in General Electric today rather than a makeup mirror, it can purchase lots of shiny new reflectors in the future.

11

Your tricycle can accompany an appropriate rider into either the men's or women's locker room without embarrassing the occupants.

12

Your bicycle will never run on and on just to hear the click of its own gears.

DON'T TRUST ANYONE
WHO TALKS ABOUT
"CUTTING EDGE"

13

Your bicycle appreciates the ride just for the sake of the ride and doesn't expect or want anything after the ride.

14

Your bicycle doesn't expect you to wax off the road tar from all of its riding before you came along.

15

Your bicycle will never accuse you of engaging in "dudsmanship" because you go to lunch with a client on a weekday rather than meet your bike for a ride.

16

Your bicycle will never assume, just because you went to lunch without it, that you were out window-shopping other bicycles – or worse, test riding them.

17

Your bicycle will never email you anything longer than one sentence.

18

Your bicycle will never write you out of its will.

19

Your bicycle will ride without worrying about whether it will have an Internet connection, a telephone, a television or a travel iron.

Your bicycle will never have more than one chin.

AH, AH, OH BABY, OH YEAH,
YEAH, A LITTLE TO THE RIGHT,
YEAH, RIGHT THERE, OH, AH, OH...

21

The mere suggestion by one bicycle that it needs to relieve itself does not trigger a chain reaction among the other bicycles at the rack that they too must relieve themselves.

22

Your bicycle will never stick its handlebars into your dinner at a restaurant and ask: "What's this you're eating?"

23

Your bicycle will never be upset because the dog sniffed you instead of it, even though it was adorned with the finest lubricant money could buy.

24

No one will ever incorrectly guess the gender of your bicycle.

25

Your bicycle will never put you through the torment of its mid-life change of gender preference.

26

Your bicycle will never retain water; and, if it does, it certainly won't tell you about it.

27

Your bicycle will never reveal what the other bicycles have under their towels in the locker room.

NO, IT COULDN'T BE... COULD IT?

28

Your bicycle will never sit on an airplane and eavesdrop.

29

Your bicycle will listen to you (and/or the hum of the road under its wheels) for hours, without interrupting you.

30

You know your bicycle is more valuable than your spouse or children, because if you file for protection under the bankruptcy laws, the trustee or receiver may take away your bicycle, but will leave you with your spouse and children – even if they have good teeth, and, even worse, if they have bad teeth!

31

Your bicycle may need maintenance, but the only disease to which your bicycle is subject is the same one that afflicts all of us as we age – rust.

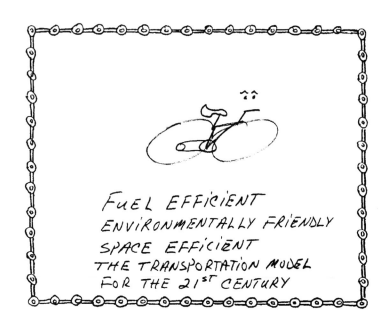

FUEL EFFICIENT
ENVIRONMENTALLY FRIENDLY
SPACE EFFICIENT
THE TRANSPORTATION MODEL
FOR THE 21ST CENTURY

September

1

If your bicycle were your work assistant, it would always be on time.

2

If your bicycle were your work assistant, it would work for lubricant.

3

If your bicycle were your work assistant, it would only want vacation for important events like riding.

4

If your bicycle were your work assistant, it would always be ready for the next climb.

5

If your bicycle were your work assistant, it would not require medical insurance, just a lubricant and a hex wrench.

6

If your bicycle were your work assistant, it would not need a pension.

7

If your bicycle were your work assistant, it would transport your customers to and from conference rooms and meetings.

8

If your bicycle were your work assistant, it would work overtime without complaint or extra pay.

9

If your bicycle were your work assistant, it would work rainy weekends.

10

After a ride, you are not obligated to call your bicycle the next day.

11

Your bicycle is a patriot. When the President says, "Let's roll," your bicycle takes him literally.

12

A safe ride with your bicycle does not mean that you avoided exposure to sexually transmitted disease.

13

Parallel parking is a snap for your bicycle.

14

Without using your hands, your bicycle still enjoys the ride.

15

Your bicycle appreciates heavy breathing.

16

Your bicycle will never be a proselytizing zealot that would wake you up on a rainy Saturday morning to preach to you.

17

Your bicycle will never get drunk – ever; but, especially, it will never get trashed at a party and announce that it only rides with you for your money, and not because of your riding form, style, and stamina.

18

Your relationship with your bicycle will never hit that awkward stage where you really don't want to ride with it, but just can't tell it so.

19

Your relationship with your bicycle will never deteriorate to the point that you are not just annoyed, but really despise:

(a) the varicose-like cracks in its paint;

(b) the smell of its grease;

(c) the way it chews road-kill;

(d) the crust on its tires;

(e) the way its ratty old seat sags; or

(f) the fact that all you can see at the breakfast table is its handlebars on either side of the morning newspaper, and it only puts the paper down to reach for its water bottle.

20

Your bicycle will never ride backwards, the wrong way, on a one-way street (unless it's a circus clown).

21

Your bicycle will never purchase chewing gum from a vending machine on its way into the restaurant.

22

Your bicycle won't keep running while you park to go into the store.

23

Your bicycle will never dress in casual khaki and then wait at the door to be picked up by the suburban (us)ault vehicle to avoid a warm summer rain.

24

Your bicycle will never ask you to take out a mortgage to buy a money pit of a house. Your bicycle is happy to hang on any wall.

25

Your bicycle will never tell you that you must buy designer linen for your bathroom – even if that's the wall it hangs on.

26

Your bicycle doesn't need a hot tub.

27

Your bicycle will never hang its dirty, ugly, fungus-infected pedals out of the window if it happens to be in your car.

28

A safe ride with your bicycle does not involve embarrassing looks from the pharmacist.

29

Your bicycle understands that "craft fairs" are inventory suppliers for garage sales.

30

Your bicycle will never complain if you hang out at the local bike shop and come home with the scent of another bicycle on your clothes.

VIRTUAL RIDE?
WHO WOULD DO THAT?
AND WHY?

October

1

You never have to explain to your bicycle why you like to ride in the morning.

2

You look good wearing tight-fitting metallic-colored clothing when you ride your bicycle.

3

You don't have to give cute names to your bicycle's parts. For example, you don't have to refer to the crank arm as "Mr. Happy".

4

You'll never be jealous of your bicycle getting more mail than you.

5

Your bicycle will always introduce you to those it rides with, and, who knows, you may develop new riding partners.

6

Your bicycle will never be upset because you pet the dog before, during or after a ride. In fact, your bicycle is very glad that you are friends with the dog.

HEY, DON'T LAUGH.
MOTHER SAYS I CAN
RECYCLE INTO ANTHING I WANT TO BE.

7

Your bicycle will never threaten to cancel your subscription when the spring issue arrives showing all the hot new models, fully accessorized.

8

When your bicycle reaches its teen years, it won't become a gangling awkward creature; instead it will continue to move with grace and poise.

9

Your bicycle will never drink and ride.

10

Your bicycle will never establish its own little fiefdom or claim turf like a bathroom, study, closet or chest of drawers for itself.

11

Your bicycle will never ask/demand that you go deep into debt to purchase a home that you can't afford and don't want, in a neighborhood with snooty, non-bicycling neighbors who drive suburban (us)ault vehicles.

12

Your bicycle will never try to trick you with some moral or ethical dilemma. For the bicycle, the only question is: "road or off-road?"

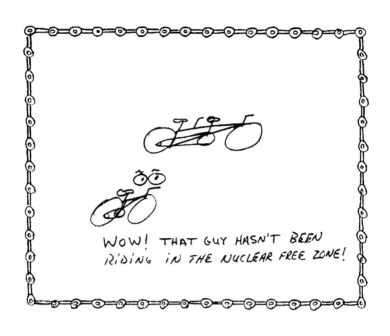

13

It's not your bicycle that complains about the hills, headwinds or holiday traffic.

14

Your bicycle doesn't come veiled in the shroud of politics or any activist group. It comes in bubble wrap.

15

Your bicycle doesn't come with any preconceived bias about the rider because of the rider's height, weight, occupation, tattoo preferences or bicycling shorts (or not).

16

Your bicycle does not know how to say: "I told you so."

17

Your bicycle will do what you ask, instead of what it thinks is a favor.

18

Your bicycle doesn't wait until after you have passed the intersection to tell you that you were supposed to turn.

19

Your bicycle won't throw away your nudist monthly.

20

Your bicycle isn't jealous of the cover model on *Bicycling Magazine*.

21

Your bicycle doesn't require that you buy the softest tissue.

22

Your bicycle never has a nubby seat post.

23

If a politician rides your bike, it's not an embarrassment to the family.

24

Unlike your daughter, you don't have to worry about whom your bike rides around with.

25

Unlike your daughter, you don't have to worry when your bike spends the night away from home.

26

Unlike your daughter, "flat" only means a new tube and not cosmetic surgery.

C'MON. YOU DON'T NEED MATCHING SOCKS.

27

Unlike your daughter, "graduation" means that the training wheels come off, not the purchase of a new car.

28

Unlike your daughter, you don't have to worry about a dirty old man riding your bicycle.

29

Unlike your daughter, your bicycle won't marry a deadbeat.

30

Unlike your daughter, if your bicycle does marry a deadbeat, you have no compunction about welcoming your bicycle back into your home and locking out the deadbeat.

31

Unlike your daughter, your bicycle won't flunk phys ed.

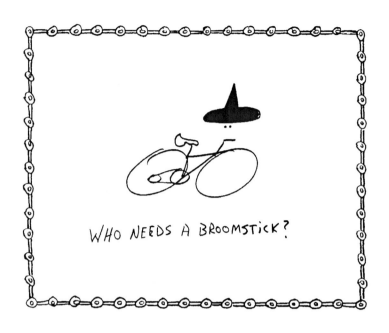

WHO NEEDS A BROOMSTICK?

November

1

You can afford driving insurance for your bicycle, unlike for your children.

2

Your bicycle won't sit around on the couch all day, eating chocolate, and watching pitiful daytime television.

3

Your bicycle doesn't make long-distance telephone calls, even to its family and friends in Italy, France, and England.

4

If your bicycle were a politician, no one would care if it rode with the interns.

5

Your bicycle will never tax your gasoline and then set the traffic lights to require that you stop at every intersection.

6

Your bicycle understands and heeds the movie preview: "Thank you for not talking during the feature presentation."

7

If your bicycle would ever be drafted to serve in public office, it would be a marvelous leader. Consider the things that your bicycle would support:

(a) Improved roads. There would be no more oil and cinder roads. Potholes would actually be paved over, not filled in to create a pot-mound instead of a pothole.

(b) Clean air.

(c) Fuel-efficient transportation.

(d) Separate parking zones for pick-up trucks and suburban (us)ault vehicles and mini-vans that bicycles can't see over or around.

(e) Roads with paved berms for pedestrians and bicycles.

8

Your bicycle is not part of gen X, gen Y or any other generation. Your bicycle is timeless and your experience with it lasts forever.

9

Your bicycle's name doesn't matter. It doesn't have to have a power name or a charming name. However badly the name is mispronounced, it is only evidence of your bicycle's class and sophistication.

10

Your bicycle won't decline a cocktail in first class and then just take a "sip" of yours.

11

Your bicycle will never pick the seam of its jeans out of its butt crack when it stands up to ride.

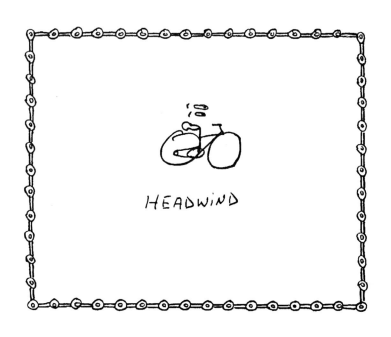

HEADWIND

12

Your bicycle won't expect you not to laugh when it tells you about a goat weed product it consumes to prevent bloating and water retention.

13

Your bicycle never changes your preset radio selections.

14

You never have to tell your bicycle to get out of the light.

15

Your bicycle will never buy you a poster of Gillian Anderson (a non-bicycle goddess) and then get mad when you frame it and hang it on the wall next to your bicycle.

16

Your bicycle may ride on the Friday after Thanksgiving, but it will never go shopping.

17

Your bicycle does not feel the need to buy Christmas presents for relatives three times removed and then stress about whether the gift is too much, too little or the wrong color.

18

Your bicycle won't telephone you at 2:45 A.M. to wake you and tell you that it is worried about the ride in the morning.

19

Your bicycle will never recommend that you deliver a peace offering "if you know what's good for you".

20

Unlike a college athlete, your bicycle:

(a) will never major in basket weaving;

(b) will never consume its weight in beer after a ride;

(c) will never overturn parked cars to celebrate a victory or protest a loss;

(d) may actually graduate.

21

Your bicycle will never complain that it is trapped inside the wrong frame.

22

Your bicycle has no need for assertiveness training. More importantly, your bicycle will never practice its assertiveness training when there are others in line behind it.

23

Your bicycle will never announce: "Yes, we're losing money, but we're losing it in an orderly manner."

24

Your bicycle will not appear on TV in obnoxious commercials for hemorrhoid cream, foot fungus powder, bad breath deodorant or lawyers.

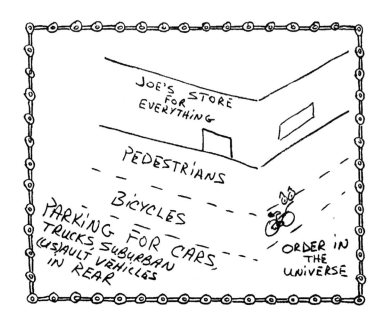

25

Your bicycle won't spend weeks planning, and days preparing, Thanksgiving dinner, and then try to convince you that instead of pure pleasure the effort was a miserable, grueling day in the sweatshop of the kitchen.

26

Your bicycle will never organize a party on a holiday when there are a thousand other events, and then become bitter when guests ride some place else.

27

Your bicycle will never block a narrow grocery store aisle to consider the pros and cons of extra-absorbent versus super-absorbent tissue.

28

You have as much anticipation of a ride with your bicycle today as you did when you and your bicycle were first introduced.

29

Your bicycle is never so intent on making a right turn on red that it misses the light turning green.

30

When your bicycle tells you that you are stuck in a rut, it means that you are caught between uneven surfaces. It is not condemning your lifestyle.

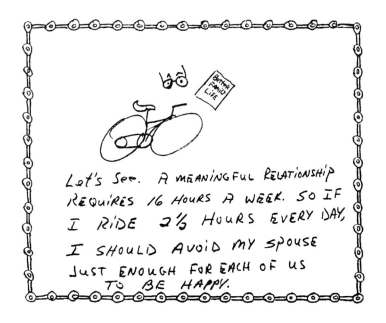

Let's see. A meaningful relationship requires 16 hours a week. So if I ride 2⅓ hours every day, I should avoid my spouse just enough for each of us to be happy.

December

1

Your bicycle won't give you instructions as to what you are allowed to say and not allowed to say at a dinner party.

2

Your bicycle will never put its chicken bones on your plate.

3

If your apartment has eight-foot ceilings, your bicycle won't buy a nine-foot Christmas tree.

4

If you already have a string of Christmas lights and a spare set, your bicycle won't buy another set each year just because they're on sale.

5

Your bicycle understands that you should be able to see some of the Christmas tree under all of the balls, bobbles, angels, garland, foil, and lights.

6

The sporting goods store is home away from home for your bicycle.

7

Your bicycle won't strap a nine-foot Christmas tree to its top tube and then try to ride home.

8

Your bicycle does not need to rent warehouse space to store its Christmas decorations.

9

Your bicycle won't have a panic attack because the Christmas tree decorations are not perfectly symmetrical.

10

Your bicycle won't buy a Christmas tree with an "S" trunk and then remind you that Christmas is its favorite holiday and if you had any Christmas spirit at all you could get the tree to stand straight.

11

Your bicycle knows that all you want on your birthday is a long enjoyable ride – fast or slow, smooth or off road – it doesn't matter, it's your birthday.

12

You don't have to dress up like a policeman or a cowboy to ride your bike.

13

Your bicycle understands that your Christmas tree doesn't need more wiring than a 747 jumbo jet.

THIS GIZMO IS HIGH TECH.
IT WILL CALCULATE MY
ARRIVAL TIME AND SEND
AHEAD FOR A COLD ONE.

14

Your bicycle won't "finish" its holiday shopping and then keep buying those things that are "stocking stuffers" or "oh so cute" or "keepsakes" or "just one more present".

15

Heavy metal? Not your bicycle!

16

Unlike a human type, your bicycle won't threaten you with bodily harm for taking notes about the funny things that it does.

17

Your bicycle will never be ejected from the stadium for using the other gender's restroom facility.

18

Your bicycle will never purchase an expensive floor-length gown with the idea that the color and style would make a wonderful mini-dress.

19

Your bicycle will never tell you that you're not half the frame of an earlier model.

20

Your bicycle will never buy three seat covers for one event with the expectation that it will make a final decision on the evening of the event and then return the two "also-rans".

I'VE GOT TO
GET A RACK

21

Your bicycle will never ask you during the week before Christmas to remodel the living room, kitchen, dining room, and guest bedroom, and then grumble because you did not completely finish the project in time for Christmas Eve entertaining.

22

You don't mind the little rubber "hairs" on your bicycle's new tires.

23

A reference to your bike as "Queen of the Road" does not imply that it is a truck-stop trollop.

24

Your bicycle has quick release wheels. There is no fumbling with snaps or hooks and loops.

25

Nothing creates the pure joy, excitement, anticipation, and thrill of seeing your bicycle under the Christmas tree. You'll get to the socks, shirts, and stocking stuffers later. Right now, you're thinking that you can navigate your bike past the dining-room table and clear the cabinet before you hit the kitchen and then...

WHAT OTHER PRESENTS?

26

Your bicycle will never ask you prepare a list of any ten things that it could do that would make you happy and afterwards inform you that it would select only those items it liked, and, if it didn't like any items on the list, you'd have to prepare another list and try again.

27

No one will think less of you because you ride alone.

28

Your bicycle doesn't use a cell phone while riding.

29

Your bicycle won't think less of you because you don't use decorated tissue covers, dishwashing bottle dispensers, and paper towels.

30

Unlike broadcast journalists, your bicycle will never try to tell you at 11 P.M. tonight what the news will be tomorrow at 6 P.M.

31

Your bicycle will never have so many accessories that it rents space at the bike shop to warehouse the out-of-season accessories and only stores the in-season gear at your apartment.

LaVergne, TN USA
19 July 2010
190061LV00001B/18/A